We love the park.

A day at the park
is a day full of fun.

The park

Dogs

Our dog Scamp loves the park.

Scamp can run and play
with the other dogs.

Scamp is so happy at the park.

When Scamp is happy, we are happy too.

That is why we love the park.

Our dog

Playing on the grass

We can run and play, too.

The grass is soft. So if we fall over, we do not get hurt.

Dad takes us to a bench to rest.

He says, "When you are happy,
I am happy too".

That is why Dad loves the park.

Bench

Our friend Mrs Brown is
sitting on the bench.

She has a bag full of bread
to feed the pigeons.

On the bench

Pigeons

Mrs Brown says she feeds the pigeons every day.

That is why she loves the park.

Feeding pigeons

Sometimes Mrs Brown
gives us some bread.

Then we feed the pigeons.

We feed the squirrel, too. It grabs the bread and runs up a tree.

Squirrel

It is fun to see a squirrel in a tree.

12

The park has many old trees.

Some trees are very tall. They grow high into the sky.

Tall trees

In the park there is a lake.

We all run towards the lake.

"Don't fall in the water!"
says Dad.

By the water

Lake

15

Near the lake there is
a family of ducks.

We see a mother duck
and five little ducklings.

Duck family

Sometimes the ducks say,
"Quack, quack, quack!" to us.

We say, "Quack, quack!" to them.

Playground

In the park there is a playground.

When we see it, we start to run.

We cannot wait to play there.

In the playground there is a seesaw.

There are lots of boys and girls to play with.

Seesaw

Sun

The sun is going down.

We know it is time to go.
But we do not want to leave.

We love the park. It is so much fun.
We never want to leave.

"Don't worry," says Dad.
"We will come back soon."

Time to go

Here are some words and phrases from the book.

Ducks swim

Dogs run

Sit on the bench

Play on the seesaw

Feed the pigeons

Squirrel

Play with the dog

Walk home

Can you use these words to write your own story?

Did you see these in the book?

Bicycle

Tail

Whiskers

Slide

© Aladdin Books Ltd 2001
All rights reserved
Designed and produced by
Aladdin Books Ltd
28 Percy Street
London W1T 2BZ
Literacy Consultant
Jackie Holderness
Printed in U.A.E.

First published in
Great Britain in 2001 by
Franklin Watts
96 Leonard Street
London EC2A 4XD

A catalogue record for this
book is available from the
British Library.

ISBN 0 7496 4839 2

Illustrator
Mary Lonsdale - SGA

Picture Credits
All photos by Select Pictures
except 4, 22b, 24tr – Digital
Stock. 20, 24tl – Stockbyte.